Tornado!

by Cynthia Pratt Nicolson

Kids Can Press

For the kids at Bowen Island Community School

Acknowledgments

Many thanks to Dr. Roger Edwards of the U.S. Storm Prediction Center who generously shared his knowledge and enthusiasm while reviewing the draft manuscript of this book. Any errors that may have crept into the final book are my responsibility. Thanks also to the capable and hard-working team at Kids Can Press, especially my editors, Stacey Roderick and Val Wyatt; photo researcher Patricia Buckley; illustrator Bill Slavin and designer Julia Naimska. I feel fortunate to work with such a dedicated, professional crew.

Kids Can Press acknowledges the financial support of the Ontario Arts Council, the Canada Council for the Arts and the Government of Canada, through the BPIDP, for our publishing activity.

Published in Canada by	Published in the U.S. by
Kids Can Press Ltd.	Kids Can Press Ltd.
29 Birch Avenue	2250 Military Road
Toronto, ON M4V 1E2	Tonawanda, NY 14150

www.kidscanpress.com

Edited by Stacey Roderick
Designed by Julia Naimska
Printed and bound in Hong Kong, China, by Book Art Inc., Toronto

The hardcover edition of this book is smyth sewn casebound.
The paperback edition of this book is limp sewn with a drawn-on cover.

CM 03 0 9 8 7 6 5 4 3 2 1
CM PA 03 0 9 8 7 6 5 4 3 2 1

National Library of Canada Cataloguing in Publication Data

Nicolson, Cynthia Pratt
Tornado! / written by Cynthia Pratt Nicolson.

(Disaster)
Includes index.
ISBN 1-55074-951-X (bound).   ISBN 1-55074-972-2 (pbk.)

1. Tornadoes — Juvenile literature. I. Title. II. Series: Disaster (Toronto, Ont.)

QC955.2.N52 2003   j551.55'3   C2002-902991-0

Photo Credits

Every reasonable effort has been made to trace ownership of and give accurate credit to copyrighted material. Information that would enable the publisher to correct any discrepancies in future editions would be appreciated.

Abbreviations
t = top; b = bottom; c = center; l = left; r = right
NOAA: National Oceanic and Atmospheric Administration

Cover Photograph: NOAA

p. 1: Messenger-Inquirer, Owensboro; **p. 3:** (t) NOAA, (b) Jeff Mitchell/Reuters NewMedia Inc./Corbis/Magma; **p. 4:** Copyright 1999, The Oklahoma Publishing Company; **p. 5:** (t) NOAA, (b) Paul Buck/AFP/Corbis/Magma; **p. 6:** Jeff Mitchell/Reuters NewMedia Inc./Corbis/Magma; **p. 7:** (t) Hector Mata/AFP/Corbis/Magma, (b) Paul Buck/AFP/Corbis/Magma; **p. 8:** NOAA; **p. 9:** NOAA; **p. 11:** NASA; **pp. 12–13:** (all) NOAA; **p. 14:** Jackson County Historical Society; **p. 15:** (t) Jackson County Historical Society, (b) NOAA; **p. 16:** (t) Hector Mata/AFP/Corbis/Magma, (b) Ray Foli/Bettmann/Corbis/Magma; **p. 17:** NOAA; **p. 18:** (t) NOAA, (b) Bettmann/Corbis/Magma; **p. 19:** Carol Huges/Gallo Images/Corbis/Magma, (b) Minnesota Historical Society and the Minneapolis Star; **p. 20:** NASA; **p. 21:** (l) Steve Simon/The Edmonton Journal, (r) Bureau of Meteorology, Australia; **p. 22:** NOAA; **p. 23:** (both) NOAA; **p. 24:** (both) NOAA; **p. 25:** (t) NOAA, (b) NASA; **p. 26:** Heritage Museum of Thurston County, Nebraska/Toronto Reference Library; **p. 27:** Corbis/Sygma/Magma; **p. 28:** (both) Messenger-Inquirer, Owensboro; **p. 29:** (t) Messenger-Inquirer, Owensboro, (b) Courtesy Big Rivers Chapter American Red Cross/Photo by Sandra Shoup; **p. 30:** Gaylon Wampler/Timepix.

Kids Can Press is a *corus*™ Entertainment company

CONTENTS

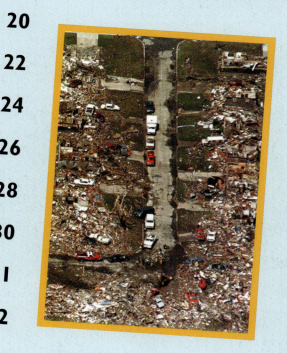

TORNADO Rips through OKLAHOMA

Warning sirens howled. Police cleared the streets, urging people to take cover. Radio and television stations cautioned everyone to hide. What was the danger? A tornado was on its way!

Late in the afternoon of May 3, 1999, weather experts predicted that a powerful tornado was about to hit the Oklahoma City area. Their warnings sent people scrambling into storm shelters, basements and closets.

High winds whip trees as a powerful tornado rips through Oklahoma City on the evening of May 3, 1999. The tornado traveled 64 km (40 mi.), rampaging through several towns on its journey of destruction.

Dark thunderclouds gave birth to this tornado and dozens of others in Oklahoma state. The storm clouds formed when warm, moist air suddenly billowed upward at the end of a hot afternoon.

The Turner family invited neighbors into their underground storm cellar. As the sky blackened, 35 people squeezed into one tiny room. Would they be safe from the blast?

Just after 7:00 P.M., the tornado roared into the southern part of Oklahoma City and the surrounding towns. As it came closer, the rumble grew louder and louder. Houses began to shake. The wild winds tore the door off the Turners' storm cellar while everyone huddled inside.

The tornado destroyed nearly everything in its path. It ripped roofs off houses and flung them aside like bits of paper. Twirling winds picked up cars and trucks and tossed them like toys.

The violence lasted for over an hour. Finally, when all was quiet, the Turners and their neighbors crawled out of the storm cellar. Their homes had been destroyed, but they had not been hurt. Everyone was glad to be alive.

Steve Lipscomb tosses a board from the pile of rubble that was his parents' home in southeast Oklahoma City. In the past, over 100 tornadoes have struck Oklahoma City, making it the most tornado-prone city in North America.

BLOWN AWAY!

Residents of the Oklahoma City area were dazed by the amount of wreckage caused by the tornado of May 3, 1999. Hundreds of homes were flattened. Trees and power poles were smashed into splinters. Twisted wire, lumber, shingles and insulation lay everywhere. Mangled toys, appliances and furniture were scattered over the ground.

"It looks like a huge battle has taken place," State Governor Frank Keating told news reporters.

Homeless families gathered in schools, churches and recreation centers. Listening to the news, they learned that their attacker had earned the "F5" label given only to the most destructive of tornadoes.

But the Oklahoma City twister had not been alone. Dozens of tornadoes had struck the states of Oklahoma and Kansas on the evening of May 3. Thousands of homes and businesses were destroyed or severely damaged. In all, the tornado outbreak killed 47 people and injured hundreds of others.

Without the warnings, experts estimate that the tornado outbreak would have killed 700 people. Things were very bad, but they could have been much worse.

Driveways and rubble are all that remain of this tornado-stricken neighborhood in Moore, Oklahoma. In total, the outbreak caused an estimated $1.2 billion in damage, making it the most costly tornado event in U.S. history.

Smashed lumber and chunks of metal appliances surround a man walking through the ruins of his home in Midwest City, Oklahoma.

Military workers sort through the wreckage of a home in Del City, Oklahoma. The house was one of thousands destroyed when Oklahoma and Kansas states were ravaged by a swarm of tornadoes on May 3, 1999.

DISASTER DATA

Tornadoes are incredibly intense, spiraling windstorms. They reach down to the ground from the clouds of enormous thunderstorms. Tornadoes can happen at any time of the year and almost anywhere on Earth, but they're most common in the central United States during spring and summer. About 1000 tornadoes zap the United States every year, while Canada is hit by about 100. Improved predictions and warnings are keeping more people safe from these violent storms.

Spawning a TWISTER

What causes a tornado like the one that tore through Oklahoma City? Scientists aren't exactly sure. In recent years, however, they have uncovered many clues to this intriguing mystery.

Most tornadoes are born from long-lasting storms called supercells. These huge thunderstorms develop where a mass of warm, moist air lies next to the ground, trapped by another warm layer called a "lid" or "cap." Because warm air is lighter than cold air, it pushes upward. Extra heat from the sun or a strong wind in the upper atmosphere may be all that's needed to open the lid.

Lightning often accompanies tornadoes. This time-lapse photo shows several flashes zapping the sky during a night-time thunderstorm. Rapid air movement within a severe storm causes ice particles to collide, creating the buildup of electrical charge that result in lightning.

As soon as it is released, the warm, moist air shoots upward through the lid and into the cold air above. It cools as it rises, causing its moisture to condense into drops of water and form enormous, billowing storm clouds. Lightning crackles and thunder growls. Rain and hail pelt down.

In most storms, the rain and hail fall directly into the rising air and the storm is soon over. A supercell, however, is different. Higher level winds push its top clouds to one side. Rain falls away from the base of the storm. The storm slowly rotates, making its own area of low pressure that forces air to rush in.

Fueled by low pressure and heat energy from the condensing water vapor, the updraft (rising flow of air) grows stronger and stronger. In some supercells, the updraft reaches speeds of 240 km/h (150 m.p.h.) and carries water vapor to levels higher than the top of Mount Everest.

Towering thunderclouds and a side-swept top are characteristics of a supercell storm. Rotating air masses inside such storms sometimes lead to the formation of tornadoes.

Near the ground, the powerful updraft draws air toward the base of the supercell. At higher levels, winds enter the storm from different directions. They may be traveling at different speeds. These variations in speed and direction are called wind shear. Wind shear causes the storm to twist and rotate.

Cold, sinking air creates downward gusts at the front and back of the supercell. As the whole storm turns, cool and warm air meet, producing a low "wall cloud" beneath the main cloud. Finally, a finger of spinning air stretches down from the wall. When it touches the earth, a tornado is born.

Huge lumps of hail, like this baseball-sized chunk, often fall from the severe thunderstorms that spawn tornadoes. Hail forms when an ice pellet rises and falls on the wet air currents inside a storm cloud, adding layer after layer of ice. Eventually, the pellet becomes too heavy and plummets to the ground as a hailstone.

YOU TRY IT

The power of warm, rising air is a key ingredient in creating tornadoes. You can observe this force with a simple experiment.

Use a plastic lid to trace a circle on a piece of paper. Beginning at the outer edge, draw a line that spirals toward the center of the circle. Make each section of your spiral about 1 cm

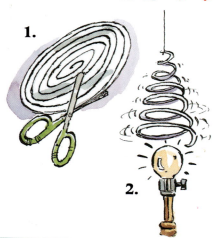

1.

2.

(1/2 in.) wide. Cut along the lines.

Knot the end of a 25 cm (10 in.) piece of thread and pull it through the center of your spiral using a sewing needle. Holding the thread, dangle your spiral above a lamp. Warm air, heated by the light bulb, rushes upward, making your spiral spin.

TOTALLY TWISTED

A spinning tornado reaches down from a rotating thunderstorm called a supercell. Tornadoes come in many shapes and sizes, but most share the features shown here.

A dark curtain of cloud hangs below the supercell. This "wall cloud" hangs low with moisture.

As the tornado touches the ground, it sends dust and debris flying. Some is lifted by the twirling vortex.

The tornado's path can grow to cover one-and-a-half kilometers (a mile) wide. In the United States, most tornadoes head in a northeast direction. They often leave a clear trail of destruction on the ground.

A swirling funnel, or vortex, drops down from the base of the storm. Its winds can reach speeds of 480 km/h (300 m.p.h.) and more. Condensed water vapor held in the vortex makes it visible.

Close to the ground, winds rush toward the low-pressure region at the center of the vortex. Near a violent tornado, these "in-flow" winds are strong enough to tear roofs off houses and toss trains from their tracks.

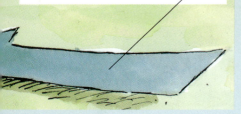

DISASTER DATA

Many people confuse tornadoes with hurricanes. Both are spiraling windstorms, but they're definitely not the same. Hurricanes are about 2000 times bigger than tornadoes. (If a tornado were the size of a small cookie, a hurricane would cover a football field.) Hurricanes last for several days, while most tornadoes last less than 10 minutes. Although hurricane winds reach a speedy 240 km/h (150 m.p.h.), tornado winds can be even faster, sometimes topping 480 km/h (300 m.p.h.).

Hurricane Andrew spins above the Atlantic Ocean before striking Florida in October 1992. Hurricanes always start out above warm ocean waters. Tornadoes usually form over land.

Birth and Death of a TORNADO

Massive storm clouds gathered over Cordell, Oklahoma, at the end of a warm afternoon on May 22, 1981. Conditions were just right for the birth of a tornado.

Winds whip up the dirt from a farmer's field as the tornado begins to form at 5:20 P.M.

Within minutes, a pointed funnel stretches down from the heavy thundercloud.

The mature tornado reaches all the way to the ground. Dust and debris continue to fly up from the farm fields below.

The tornado stretches into a long, thin "rope" as it begins to die out.

At 5:28 P.M. the vortex disappears. From start to finish, the tornado has lasted less than 10 minutes.

You Try It

A tornado spins faster as it becomes more tightly twisted, just as a figure skater twirls faster by pulling in her arms. You can feel this effect by sitting on a revolving chair or stool and holding a heavy book in each hand. Extend your

arms straight out to the sides. Now ask a friend to start spinning you slowly.

As you spin, quickly pull the books tightly against your body. What happens? Like a tornado, the more compact you are, the faster you spin.

TRI-STATE TERROR

The midday sky suddenly darkened over Annapolis, Missouri, on March 18, 1925. Moments later, a boiling cloud of dust and debris charged over the nearby hills. At the cloud's center was a huge tornado that quickly devoured the tiny town. The deadliest tornado in U.S. history had just begun.

A Chicago newspaper headline tells of the disastrous tornado that struck Missouri, Illinois and Indiana on March 18, 1925. While the death toll has since been revised to 695, the Tri-State Tornado is still on record as the deadliest tornado in U.S. history.

The tornado roared across the Mississippi River into the neighboring state of Illinois. Like a giant bully, it pushed straight ahead, mowing down everything in its path. The twister destroyed schools, miners' cottages, farms and villages. It smashed the town of Murphysboro, killing 234 people.

When the storm hit West Frankfort, Illinois, most of the men were working in an underground coal mine. The tornado knocked out power, leaving the miners in darkness and without an elevator. They climbed the hundreds of steps to the surface, only to find that many had lost their wives, children and homes.

The tornado turned slightly to the north as it headed into Indiana, the third state on its route. It plowed through several more farms and villages before it began to weaken. Finally, after a reign of terror lasting more than three hours, the monster tornado quietly faded away.

Altogether, the Tri-State Tornado killed almost 700 people. Some meteorologists now believe it was not a single tornado, but a "family" of related twisters, all spawned by one thunderstorm. With its incredibly long path of destruction, this storm earned the title "Tornado of the Century."

Shattered doors, walls, roofs and window frames lie jumbled together in the destroyed town of Murphysboro, Illinois. Half the town's population was killed or injured by the 1925 tornado.

Empty windows stare out from the ruins of Longfellow School in Murphysboro. The record-breaking Tri-State Tornado traveled across the Mississippi River and along a slight ridge for 350 km (217 mi.). Its average forward speed was 116 km/h (73 m.p.h.).

Rating
THE RAMPAGE

Most tornadoes come and go so quickly that it's hard to measure them. One way to figure out a tornado's strength is by looking at the mess it leaves behind.

In 1971, Dr. Theodore Fujita created a scale to rank tornadoes from zero to five. This classification system is named the Fujita Scale after its inventor.

The Fujita scale gives scientists a way to estimate a tornado's wind speed by inspecting the wreckage left after the storm. These estimates aren't exact because so much depends on where the tornado struck and the type of buildings it hit.

Heavy sheets of metal wrap around a tree stripped bare by the F5 tornado that struck Oklahoma City on May 3, 1999. In a strong tornado, such pieces are flung about as though they weighed no more than the pages of a newspaper.

Dr. Theodore Fujita observes a simulated tornado in his lab at the University of Chicago. Fujita invented the scale that ranks tornadoes from F0 to F5, according to the damage they produce.

The Fujita scale describes tornadoes as F0, F1, F2 and so on. F0 and F1 tornadoes are considered "weak," F2 and F3 are classified as "strong," and F4 and F5 are categorized as "violent."

F0 tornadoes cause relatively light damage. They break branches off trees, knock bricks off chimneys and topple signs. An F0 tornado has winds that are slower than 116 km/h (73 m.p.h.).

F1 twisters peel shingles off roofs. They can push mobile homes off their foundations and may even turn them over. F1 tornadoes blow cars off roads. Their wind speeds range from 116 km/h to 180 km/h (73 m.p.h. to 112 m.p.h.).

F2 storms create considerable damage. They tear roofs off houses and destroy mobile homes. In an F2 tornado, large trees are uprooted and cars are lifted off the ground. F2 winds range from 181 km/h to 252 km/h (113 m.p.h. to 157 m.p.h.).

F3 tornadoes produce severe damage. They can overturn trains and throw automobiles a short distance through the air. These strong twisters tear the roofs and some walls off well-built houses. Their winds range from 253 km/h to 331 km/h (158 m.p.h. to 206 m.p.h.).

F4 tornadoes cause devastating damage. They can level well-built houses and turn large objects such as bathtubs into flying missiles. The winds of an F4 tornado blow at 332 km/h to 418 km/h (207 m.p.h. to 260 m.p.h.).

F5 tornadoes generate incredible damage. They lift strong frame houses off their foundations and sweep them away. In a F5 twister, cars fly farther than 100 m (109 yd.). F5 winds range from 419 km/h to over 480 km/h (261 m.p.h. to over 300 m.p.h.).

Twin funnels threaten Elkhart, Indiana, on April 11, 1965. Theodore Fujita studied aerial photos of damage caused by this Palm Sunday tornado outbreak and discovered that more than one vortex can belong to the same tornado.

YOU TRY IT

You'll often read that a tornado "sucks up" debris, but this isn't accurate. In fact, debris is swirled into the air by a tornado's winds. You can see this lifting action for yourself.

Fill a tall, clear container with water. Open a teabag and stir the loose tea leaves into the water. Now let the

mixture sit until all the leaves have settled to the bottom.

With a small spoon, gently stir the top of the water. Continue to stir as you watch what happens to the "debris" at the bottom of the container. You'll see it rise into a twirling funnel, with no suction required.

WEIRD and WONDERFUL

Although they cause terrible disasters, tornadoes also inspire some amusing — and amazing — stories. Some, like the tale of a twister that turned an iron pot inside out, are definitely beyond belief. Other reports are strange but apparently true.

John Lewis of Mountain Ash, England, was astounded one day in February 1859. As he later recounted, "Something was falling all over me, down my neck, on my head, and on my back. They were little fish. I saw the whole ground covered with them." Apparently, a waterspout (a tornado over water) had lifted the fish from a nearby lake and dropped them on Lewis's town.

In a similar story, citizens of Marksville, Louisiana, woke to find their yards, streets and roofs covered with fish on October 23, 1947. Other places have reported ducks, frogs, snails and salamanders dropping from the clouds. In spite of the old saying, no one has reported that it has rained cats and dogs.

This waterspout off the Florida Keys was photographed from an aircraft in 1969. Although waterspouts are usually smaller and weaker than land tornadoes, they can flip small boats and damage ships.

It's time to sleep elsewhere when a tornado has flipped your house onto its side. A 1950 tornado in LaPorte, Texas, not only knocked this house over, it also dragged the building sideways for 23 m (75 ft.).

Every year, tornadoes carry light objects such as letters and photographs for 48 km (30 mi.) or more. A personal check soared 375 km (233 mi.) from Stockton, Kansas, to Winnetoon, Nebraska, on April 11, 1991. That twister-delivered piece of airmail holds the record for the farthest-flung piece of debris.

Tornadoes can carry heavy objects long distances as well. For instance, a motel sign from Broken Bow, Oklahoma, was carried 48 km (30 mi.) and dropped in Arkansas on April 2, 1982. A very strong tornado can carry a car for almost a kilometer (half a mile).

People and animals can be picked up by tornadoes but they often do not survive their journeys. One exception was nine-year-old Sharon Weron who was scooped up by a tornado on July 1, 1955. After flying about 300 m (1000 ft.), Sharon landed safely on her tummy and got her worst injuries when lumps of hail hit her on the head.

A dust devil swirls skyward in Namibia, Africa. Dust devils look like small tornadoes but they form differently — when hot air rises above sun-baked ground.

There are many tornado stories of chickens, like the one shown here, that have been plucked by a tornado. One explanation is that a chicken's feathers become loose when it is frightened and are easily blown off by the tornado's strong winds.

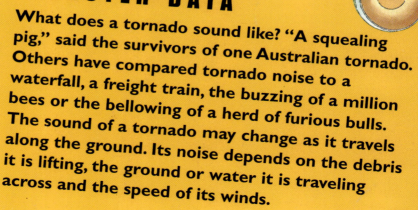

DISASTER DATA

What does a tornado sound like? "A squealing pig," said the survivors of one Australian tornado. Others have compared tornado noise to a waterfall, a freight train, the buzzing of a million bees or the bellowing of a herd of furious bulls. The sound of a tornado may change as it travels along the ground. Its noise depends on the debris it is lifting, the ground or water it is traveling across and the speed of its winds.

DOING DAMAGE AROUND THE WORLD

The world's most deadly tornadoes have struck the country of Bangladesh, shown in this satellite photo. Scientists are studying the haze of pollution that covers Bangladesh and nearby northern India to find out how it affects both local and global weather.

Experts estimate that approximately 1500 tornadoes twist and turn across Earth's surface each year. More than half of these spin over an area nicknamed Tornado Alley in the central United States. Here dry west winds and cool north winds blow above warm, moist air from the Gulf of Mexico. The unstable weather conditions produce supercell thunderstorms and tornadoes.

While North American storms receive lots of attention, some of the worst tornadoes of all time have struck on the other side of the planet. The most deadly tornado ever recorded hit the country of Bangladesh on April 26, 1989. Officials estimated that the violent twister killed about 1300 people. Its wide path of destruction extended about 80 km (50 mi.) north and northwest of Dhaka and left about 80 000 people homeles

Seven years later, another severe tornado ripped throu northern Bangladesh. In a country where many people live close together in fragile

A huge tornado rips through Edmonton, Alberta, on the afternoon of July 31, 1987. The twister stayed on the ground for an hour, killing 27 people, injuring hundreds of others and destroying more than 300 homes. The Edmonton tornado was one of the worst natural disasters in Canadian history.

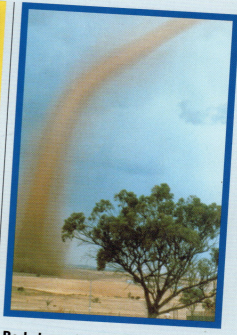

Red dust tints the funnel of this colorful tornado near Northam, Australia. Because the tornado remained in open country, it caused no deaths or injuries and little property damage.

homes, the tornado flattened about 80 villages in less than 30 minutes. It left about 500 dead and hospitals overflowing with the nearly 50 000 injured.

Meteorologists think that Bangladesh is tornado-prone for some of the same reasons the central United States is. Warm, moist air flows into the region from the Bay of Bengal, while cold, dry air blows down from the Himalaya Mountains. The two air masses collide, creating the severe weather that gives rise to tornadoes. By comparing tornado formation in the two countries, scientists may be able to learn more about how these violent storms take shape.

Tornadoes appear in a surprising variety of places around the world. They hit Australia, Africa, Europe, Asia and South America, but the number of deaths is usually small. No one knows for sure how many tornadoes happen worldwide because few countries count their tornadoes as carefully as Canada and the United States do.

DISASTER DATA

The worst tornado outbreak ever recorded in North America struck 13 states in just over 16 hours on April 3 and 4, 1974. Called the Super Outbreak, the wild weather system spawned 148 tornadoes, including six that reached F5 intensity. The rampage stretched from Mississippi north to Michigan, and from Illinois east to Virginia, and entered Canada when one tornado hit southern Ontario. In all, 330 people were killed and over 5000 others injured.

ON THE TRAIL OF A TWISTER

Steer clear of a tornado? Not the storm chasers! These extreme-weather watchers spend long days driving around the central United States trying to get up close to a twister.

Some people chase tornadoes for fun and excitement, out of personal interest or to take photographs. Others, like Erik Rasmussen and his colleagues at the National Severe Storms Laboratory in Norman, Oklahoma, track down storms for more serious reasons. Their project, VORTEX (Verification of the Origins of Rotation in Tornadoes Experiment), was designed to investigate how tornadoes form.

Storm-chasing scientists were thrilled when this tornado touched down just south of Dimmitt, Texas, on June 2, 1995. At the time, their detailed observations made it the most studied twister in history. By learning more about how tornadoes form, scientists hope to save lives by improving tornado predictions and warnings.

In 1994 and 1995, VORTEX scientists spent several weeks chasing severe storms. They hit the roads in a fleet of vans and cars equipped with cameras and weather-sensing instruments. The researchers hoped to surround a storm and record a complete tornado life cycle, from start to finish.

Many days, the scientists were disappointed. They drove for hours without coming close to a tornado. But June 2, 1995, was different. That morning, the team gathered for their usual meeting. After hearing the day's forecast of thunderstorms, they headed west.

By mid-afternoon, the fleet of vans and cars reached western Texas. Then the scientists waited. At about 6 P.M. they learned that a storm was brewing near the town of Friona. The team rushed toward the area, only to find their way blocked by fallen

Scientists Bob Davies-Jones, Jerry Straka and Erik Rasmussen plan their next move in a VORTEX vehicle. The VORTEX fleet included several cars and vans equipped with sensors to measure temperature, humidity, winds and air pressure every six seconds.

power lines and overturned trucks. A violent tornado was in progress, but rain and blowing dust made it nearly impossible to see.

Was it time to give up for the day? No! The team headed south where another supercell was building. Finally, around

A member of the VORTEX team films a severe thunderstorm in Texas while equipment on the car roof measures weather conditions. Scientists collect storm data so that they can figure out which storms are most likely to produce tornadoes.

8 P.M., near Dimmitt, Texas, the VORTEX crew was rewarded. As their cameras clicked and weather instruments gathered data, a powerful tornado touched down right in front of them. As one researcher later wrote, "It was an awesome sight!"

You Try It

You can create a tornado-like vortex for close-up viewing. You'll need two large, clear plastic pop bottles, water, food coloring, a small plastic plumbing washer and some duct tape.

Fill one of the bottles with water and add two drops of food coloring. Place the washer on the opening of the bottle. Turn the other bottle upside-

down over the first and secure it tightly with duct tape. Over a sink or paper towel, flip the device so that the full bottle is on top. Now rotate the top bottle in a circle. Watch closely.

You will soon see a vortex forming in the tinted water. Hold the top bottle still and watch as your twister funnels down. Flip the bottles and watch again.

"Forget the mastodon! Run to the cave!" In the past, a tornado warning could be given only after someone spotted a tornado. Often, that was too late. Over the past few decades, however, meteorologists have learned how to predict many tornadoes before they form. These improved forecasts depend on new technology and better understanding of how tornadoes are created.

POWERFUL PREDICTIONS

Satellites orbiting Earth gather images of storms and air movement. Weather balloons measure temperature, humidity and pressure at mid-level altitudes. Ground-based weather instruments make surface observations. Doppler radar (which is also used by police to nab speeders) allows scientists to measure the speed of moving clouds.

All this data is fed into computers and analyzed with programs that model what happens during a storm. By adding the direct observations of trained storm spotters and storm chasers, scientists can often tell if a weather system is developing into a supercell storm. They must then monitor the situation closely to figure out whether the supercell is brewing up a tornado.

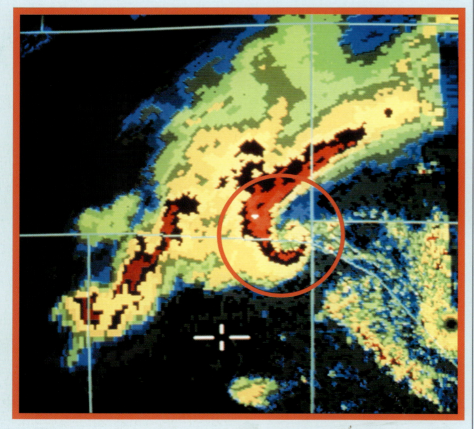

A radar image shows the "hook echo" pattern that often identifies tornado activity. Scientists depend on radar to help them figure out what's going on inside a storm.

A large military plane was destroyed when a tornado struck Tinker Air Force Base on March 25, 1948. Meteorologists at the base successfully predicted the tornado and made the world's first broadcast of a tornado warning.

When conditions indicate severe weather, the U.S. Storm Prediction Center in Norman, Oklahoma, issues a "tornado watch." Local U.S. National Weather Service offices issue a "tornado warning" when thunderstorms have developed and tornadoes look very likely. Radio, television, telephones, outdoor sirens and the Internet help get the message to the public quickly. With enough time, nearly everyone can be warned of the danger.

Tornadoes are still tough to predict, and many people continue to ignore weather warnings. Even so, the average number of people killed by tornadoes in North America has dropped dramatically since the 1920s and 1930s. Improved predictions and earlier warnings have saved many lives.

Glowing pink in the evening sun, a mature tornado hovers near Union City, Oklahoma, on May 24, 1973. This tornado was the first to be caught on Doppler radar by the scientists and storm chasers of the U.S. National Severe Storms Laboratory.

rocket launches into space rom Cape Canaveral on May 3, 000. It is carrying GOES-L a Geostationary Operational nvironmental Satellite) into rbit 35 785 km (22 240 mi.) ove Earth's surface. Weather tellites help meteorologists ck tornadoes and other ngerous weather conditions.

DISASTER DATA

Watch or warning — what's the difference? A tornado watch is issued by weather experts when tornadoes are possible in your area. Make sure you know where the closest safe place is located, and listen to the radio or television for further developments.

A tornado warning is issued when a tornado has been sighted or indicated by weather radar. The tornado could strike at any minute! When you hear a warning, it's time to go immediately to the safest part of your home and wait there until the danger has passed.

TAKE COVER!

On the afternoon of September 18, 1928, Dale Larson, 17, spotted a tornado headed toward a small schoolhouse near his family's Nebraska farm. With no time to lose, Dale drove to the school. He burst through the school door and yelled at everyone to get into the storm cellar. Moments later, an incredible roar filled the air. After the sound died down, the frightened group waited ten minutes. Then they ventured outside.

The schoolhouse had vanished. The survivors found nothing but pieces of the school's foundation, a water pump and posts from the swing. Without Dale's warning, the children and their teacher certainly would have been killed. Instead, the young man's brave, quick actions saved 30 lives.

Dale's warning worked because the school had a storm cellar where the group could take cover. If you live in a tornado-prone zone, learn which part of your home will be safest in a storm. An underground storm cellar or basement is usually best. If you have no basement, use an inner hallway or a smaller inner room without windows, such as a bathroom or closet.

Dale Larson (far left) stands with the class he saved, on the site of their former school in Thurston County, Nebraska. The entrance to the school's storm cellar, where the group took shelter, is on the lower left-hand side of this photo.

While no building is tornado-proof, a house or larger building can be made tornado-resistant. By attaching roofs to walls with metal straps, bolting walls to foundations, and bracing exterior walls, builders create structures that will stand up to all but the fiercest tornado winds. In addition to strengthening regular walls, some home-owners have made safe rooms encased in steel and concrete. Some communities have built tornado-resistant shelters for neighborhoods.

FEMA (the U.S. Federal Emergency Management Agency) has these tips for anyone caught in a tornado.

• If you are indoors, go at once to the safest part of the building. Find a place away from windows.

• Get under a sturdy piece of furniture such as a table. Use your arms to cover your head and neck.

• If you are outdoors, try to find shelter in a nearby building.

• Do not stay in a parked car or mobile home.

• If you cannot get inside a building, lie in a ditch or low-lying area.

Powerful tornado winds stripped this car and left it tangled in a tree. Emergency officials recommend that, instead of staying in a parked vehicle, you find shelter in a building or low-lying ditch during a tornado.

You Try It

Many houses lose their roofs or get blown off their foundations when a tornado strikes. You can demonstrate how reinforced construction helps a house stand up to strong winds. Fold three index cards in half and tape two of them together to make the walls of a model house. Lay the third card on

top of the walls to make a roof. Now use a hair dryer to blow on your structure. What happens? Rebuild your model using tape to anchor the walls to your desk or table and to attach the roof to the walls. Blow again to test your reinforced, tornado-resistant house.

Tornado Strikes
CITY SURVIVES

January 3, 2000, seemed like a quiet winter day in Owensboro, Kentucky. As residents chatted over lunch, some remarked on the unusually warm winter weather. No one realized that Mother Nature had a bigger surprise in store.

By mid-afternoon the temperature reached 16°C (60°F), very warm for the middle of winter. Anyone who happened to tune into a weather report heard that the National Weather Service had issued a tornado watch. Still, most people just went about their daily routines.

Then, at 3:43 P.M., the warning sirens began to blare. To find out what was going on, residents turned on their radios or televisions. They heard that the tornado watch had changed to a warning. It was time to hide!

Cleaning up after a tornado is hard work, as this Owensboro resident discovered when a twister hit her city. Tornado warnings saved many lives by giving residents nearly 30 minutes to seek shelter.

A boy and girl rescue some of their possessions from the shambles of their home in Owensboro, Kentucky. On January 3, 2000, an F3 tornado hit the city and damaged over 900 homes and businesses.

All over the city, residents sought shelter. In one bank, staff crowded into the vault where the safety deposit boxes and cash were kept. At 4:10 P.M., a powerful tornado moved into Owensboro. Within a few minutes, the power went out. In the bank, workers heard an enormous crash. The ceiling over their work space had collapsed.

An F3 tornado struck Owensboro that day. The storm destroyed over 100 homes and damaged 800 others. In all, the tornado caused millions of dollars in property damage.

In spite of all the devastation, fewer than 20 people received serious injuries and no one was killed. The warnings given by the National Weather Service saved many lives that warm winter day.

An aerial photo shows the remains of a church demolished by the Owensboro tornado. Although property damage reached an estimated $70 million, fewer than 20 people were injured and no one was killed.

A toilet bowl is all that's left of a three-bedroom home in Owensboro, Kentucky. Many residents found temporary shelter in a local sports center after the first tornado to strike the area in 200 years.

FACING THE FUTURE

Tornadoes are frightening and fascinating. They shock us with their violence and amaze us with their strength. Although scientists still puzzle over the details of how tornadoes work, their understanding has grown in recent years.

Meteorologists now use modern technology to make earlier predictions about where and when a tornado will occur. Extra warning time gives people a better chance to find a safe place to hide from a twister's wild winds. Improved forecasts, combined with modern communications, have lowered tornado death rates in North America. Unfortunately, other parts of the world continue to suffer vast losses when tornadoes strike without warning.

In the future, tornadoes will continue to surprise us with their awesome power. We still have a lot to learn about nature's fiercest winds.

Lauren Harwell, 10, shoots at a basketball hoop that was left standing when a 1992 tornado ripped through her neighborhood in Channelview, Texas. Like many tornado-struck communities, Channelview was successfully rebuilt after the storm.

Glossary

Air pressure: the pushing force of air weighing down on a particular place

Atmosphere: the layer of air surrounding Earth

Doppler radar: a system that uses reflected signals to measure the position and movement of distant objects. Meteorologists use Doppler radar to track storms.

Dust devil: a small, spinning wind that raises dust from the ground on a hot day. Dust devils are not tornadoes.

Fujita scale: a ranking of tornado strength and destructiveness, from category F0 to F5

Hurricane: a vast, spinning storm with winds over 119 km/h (74 m.p.h.)

Inflow winds: air rushing toward the low-pressure area at the center of a tornado

Meteorologist: a scientist who studies the weather

Storm cellar: an underground room that provides a safe place to hide from a tornado

Supercell: a huge, long-lasting type of thunderstorm. Most tornadoes are produced by supercells.

Tornado: a spinning wind funnel reaching down to the ground from a thunderstorm

Tornado warning: a strong caution from weather experts that a tornado could strike any minute

Tornado watch: advice from weather experts that a tornado may occur within the next few hours

Twister: a nickname for a tornado

Updraft: an upward wind produced when warm air rises

Vortex: a mass of whirling liquid or gas. A tornado is a vortex of air.

Wall cloud: a dense, moisture-filled cloud that hangs below the main clouds of a thunderstorm

Waterspout: a tornado that forms over a lake, ocean or river, lifting water into its vortex

Water vapor: tiny droplets of water in the air

Index